26th International Conference on Computational Linguistics (COLING 2016)

Tutorial Abstracts

Osaka, Japan
11 – 16 December 2016

ISBN: 978-1-5108-3338-8

Printed from e-media with permission by:

Curran Associates, Inc.
57 Morehouse Lane
Red Hook, NY 12571

Some format issues inherent in the e-media version may also appear in this print version.

Printed by Curran Associates, Inc. (2017)

Association for Computational Linguistics
209 N. Eighth Street
Stroudsburg, Pennsylvania 18360

Phone: 1-570-476-8006
Fax: 1-570-476-0860

acl@aclweb.org

Additional copies of this publication are available from:

Curran Associates, Inc.
57 Morehouse Lane
Red Hook, NY 12571 USA
Phone: 845-758-0400
Fax: 845-758-2633
Email: curran@proceedings.com
Web: www.proceedings.com

COLING 2016

The 26th International Conference on Computational Linguistics

Proceedings of COLING 2016: Tutorial Abstracts

December 11-16, 2016
Osaka, Japan

Preface: General Chair

Welcome to COLING 2016 – the 26th International Conference on Computational Linguistics — held in Osaka, Japan! It is the third COLING in Japan after Tokyo (1980) and Kyoto (1994). It is a special pleasure for me to be General Chair (10 years after chairing the joint COLING-ACL 2006 in Sydney) of a COLING held in Japan, a country I love.

COLING is organised under the auspices of the International Committee on Computational Linguistics (ICCL, http://nlp.shef.ac.uk/iccl/index.html). ICCL is a very special committee, with no fixed rules and no funding, whose only function is to make sure that a COLING appears every two years and that it is a good and friendly conference.

I have participated to many COLINGs, since the one in Pisa in 1973. It was a COLING without email! I still remember when Antonio Zampolli (Local chair) received by Hans Karlgren (Program chair) a sketch of the program written by hand, almost unreadable, and asked me (very young at the time) to interpret it. I have seen COLINGs where submissions arrived on paper and many packages were sent around the world to area chairs, to be sent to reviewers, and all the results back again by normal mail. It seems impossible now.

COLING has changed over the years, together with the changes in our field. But it has always been important for ICCL to maintain the COLING "spirit": we always wanted COLING to be an inclusive and broad conference. We also want to underline that in our field "language" is important and we therefore pay special attention to having papers and workshops focusing on understanding language properties and complexities. Moreover, for us the social part of the conference is as important as the scientific one.

An outstanding competent and dedicated team has worked for the organisation of COLING 2016. I wish to warmly thank, also on behalf of ICCL, all the various Chairs, too many to mention them all here, for the wonderful work they have done. It has been a pleasure and a privilege for me to work together with all of them: they made my work as General chair very easy. But I owe a special thanks to Yuji Matsumoto and Rashmi Prasad, Program chairs, for their hard work in managing so smoothly an impressive number of submissions, many more than we expected. And I wish to express my deepest gratitude to the Local chairs – Eiichiro Sumita, Takenobu Tokunaga and Sadao Kurohashi – who have done a fantastic work with great dedication in all the various phases of the conference organisation, always keeping everything under control. Not an easy task, as I know too well!

I also want to thank the generosity of all the sponsors for their great support to COLING.

Last but not least, I thank the colleagues (so many) who submitted their work to COLING, the organisers of Workshops and Tutorials, the participants (more than 900 at the time of writing) and the many students among them. It is important that many young researchers can attend COLINGs. They show the great interest of our community in COLING.

I hope that you benefit not only from the scientific programme but also from the social parts of COLING. I hope you get from this COLING both new exciting ideas and also new friends.

Enjoy COLING 2016 in Japan!

Nicoletta Calzolari (ICCL, ILC-CNR and ELRA)

Preface: Program Chairs

It is with great pleasure that we welcome you to the 26th International Conference on Computational Linguistics (COLING 2016) in Osaka, Japan! COLING covers a broad spectrum of technical areas related to natural language and computation. This year, we received 1,039 valid submissions (from a total of 1127 submissions), of which we accepted 337 papers (32.4% acceptance rate). 134 papers were selected for oral presentation and 203 papers for poster presentation. No distinction is made in these proceedings between papers presented orally or as a poster, as they were not distinguished qualitatively but rather by judging the best mode for delivering the paper content.

To effectively cover the broad spectrum of topics included in the conference, we have 18 thematic areas, each chaired by two or more area chairs. We are extremely grateful to the area chairs, who led and monitored the reviewing and reviewer discussions, and sent us detailed recommendation reports resulting from the reviewing process, including best paper recommendations. We cannot thank enough the over 800 reviewers who have put in the requisite time and effort to carefully assess the very large number of submissions we received this year. Their dedication and commitment, and willingness to work with us even when there were tight time constraints, made the entire task proceed much more smoothly than we had hoped! Almost all papers were reviewed by at least three reviewers and we are very happy with the highly strong set of papers accepted for presentation. We thank all authors for their submissions describing their very commendable research, and hope that authors of papers we could not accept have nevertheless benefited from the feedback they received from reviewers.

We have structured the accepted submissions into ten sessions, with multiple thematic areas included in parallel, either for oral presentation or poster presentation. Only one session – the first session – does not have a parallel poster session. We are delighted to have four invited speakers to the conference: Joakim Nivre from Uppsala University: "Universal Dependencies – Dubious Linguistics and Crappy Parsing?"; Reiko Mazuka from RIKEN Brain Science Institute & Duke University: "Getting the Input Right: Refining our Understanding of What Children Hear"; Dina Demner-Fushman from the U.S. National Library of Medicine: "NLP to support clinical tasks and decisions", and Simone Teufel from University of Cambridge: "A Look at Computational Argumentation and Summarisation from a Text-Understanding Perspective".

We are extremely grateful to the members of the best paper committee, Tim Baldwin, Vincent Ng, and Hinrich Schütze, who agreed to put in extra time to select the two best papers at the conference. Best paper nominations were collected in a bottom-up fashion, with reviewers first providing their recommendation for each paper, and area chairs then collecting the positive recommendations, and upon their own assessment of the corresponding reviews and papers, selecting some or all to be forwarded to the PC chairs. PC chairs then invited the three experts to form a committee (chaired by the PC chairs) to select the two best papers from this set of nominated papers.

We would like to thank the many members of the organizing committee who have helped us in crucial ways at various stages of organizing the technical program – the General Chair, Nicoletta Calzolari; the Local Chairs, Eiichiro Sumita, Takenobu Tokunaga and Sadao Kurohashi; the Publication Chairs, Hitoshi Isahara and Masao Utiyama; the Publicity Chairs, Srinivas Bangalore, Dekai Wu and Antonio Branco; and the Web Master Akifumi Yoshimoto. Our special thanks go to Swapna Somasundaran for her voluntary help to recruit additional reviewers to handle the much larger than expected submissions to the conference. Last but not the least, we are grateful to the softconf manager, Rich Gerber, for his continuous help with our various questions and needs.

We hope that you enjoy the conference!

Yuji Matsumoto, Nara Institute of Science and Technology, Japan
Rashmi Prasad, University of Wisconsin-Milwaukee, U.S.A.

Preface: Local Chairs

Welcome to the COLING 2016!

It is a pleasure to welcome you to COLING 2016 organized by the Japanese Association of Natural Language Processing (ANLP) in Osaka. It has been 22 years since Japan last held the conference. While we are meeting here to discuss NLP, there is no substitute for personal contact. Therefore, we have arranged breaks, a reception, an excursion and a delightful banquet to facilitate discussion, collaboration and making connections. We hope and the modern conference venue together with the ambience of western Japan including Osaka, Nara and Kyoto (famous for their nature, culture, history, and food), help to make this an enjoyable experience for all. We hope the conference will result in accelerated growth of NLP.

Organizing a conference always takes a lot of work, and fortunately, we have experienced people from all around the world in attendance at the COLING 2016 site. It is both an honor and a great pleasure to work with them, and we thank them gratefully.

Since the proposal to host COLING was accepted by ICCL in 2014, our world has experienced some drastic changes. Under unfavorable economic conditions in Japan and considering the distance from Europe and America, we had to make a very conservative financial plan for the conference. The sponsorship chairs worked very hard and collected 33 sponsors, which is considerably more than in previous COLINGs.

This year's conference has attracted a huge number of submissions and has a high level of participation, reflecting the ongoing dynamism in artificial intelligence around the globe. We were both overwhelmed by the numbers of visa applications we had to handle, and at the same time delighted and excited by the tremendous response.

We'd like to end by reporting two special features of COLING 2016: (1) COLING will assist student participants with registration subsidies. Successful applicants for the Student Support Program will receive all-inclusive free registration; (2) the collocation of the first international symposium for young researchers working on Natural Language Processing (YRSNLP) as an official satellite event at COLING 2016.

Welcome, and enjoy the conference!

Eiichiro SUMITA, Takenobu TOKUNAGA, and Sadao KUROHASHI

COLING 2016 Local Chairs

Organisers

General Chair

Nicoletta Calzolari

Programme Chairs

Yuji Matsumoto

Rashmi Prasad

Local Chairs

Eiichiro Sumita

Takenobu Tokunaga

Sadao Kurohashi

Workshops Chairs

Key-Sun Choi

Monica Monachini

Yusuke Miyao

Demo Chair

Hideo Watanabe

Tutorial Chairs

Marcello Federico

Akiko Aizawa

Publication Chairs

Hitoshi Isahara

Masao Utiyama

Sponsorship Chairs

Satoshi Sekine

Su Jian

Patrick Pantel

Chengqing Zong

Ralf Steinberger

Publicity Chairs

Srinivas Bangalore

Dekai Wu

Antonio Branco

Advisor to the Local Committee

John Judge

Web Master

Akifumi Yoshimoto

Student Volunteer Coordinator

Yugo Murawaki

Program Booklet Coordinator

Akihiro Tamura

Table of Contents

Conference Program

Sunday December 11, 2016

09:00–12:00 T-1

Compositional Distributional Models of Meaning
Mehrnoosh Sadrzadeh and Dimitri Kartsaklis

09:00–12:00 T-2

Chinese Textual Sentiment Analysis: Datasets, Resources and Tools
Lun-Wei Ku and Wei-Fan Chen

14:00–17:00 T-3

Natural Language Processing for Intelligent Access to Scientific Information
Horacio Saggion and Francesco Ronzano

14:00–17:00 T-4

Quality Estimation for Language Output Applications
Carolina Scarton, Gustavo Paetzold and Lucia Specia

Monday December 12, 2016

09:00–12:00 **T-5**

Translationese: Between Human and Machine Translation
Shuly Winter

09:00–12:00 **T-6**

Succinct Data Structures for NLP-at-Scale
Matthias Petri and Trevor Cohn

14:00–17:00 **T-7**

The Role of Wikipedia in Text Analysis and Retrieval
Marius Pasca

Compositional Distributional Models of Meaning

Mehrnoosh Sadrzadeh **Dimitri Kartsaklis**

Queen Mary University of London
School of Electronic Engineering and Computer Science
Mile End Road, London E1 4NS, UK
{mehrnoosh.sadrzadeh;d.kartsaklis}@qmul.ac.uk

1 Description

Distributional models of meaning (see Turney and Pantel (2010) for an overview) are based on the pragmatic hypothesis that meanings of words are deducible from the contexts in which they are often used. This hypothesis is formalized using vector spaces, wherein a word is represented as a vector of co-occurrence statistics with a set of context dimensions. With the increasing availability of large corpora of text, these models constitute a well-established NLP technique for evaluating semantic similarities. Their methods however do not scale up to larger text constituents (i.e. phrases and sentences), since the uniqueness of multi-word expressions would inevitably lead to data sparsity problems, hence to unreliable vectorial representations. The problem is usually addressed by the provision of a compositional function, the purpose of which is to prepare a vector for a phrase or sentence by combining the vectors of the words therein. This line of research has led to the field of compositional distributional models of meaning (CDMs), where reliable semantic representations are provided for phrases, sentences, and discourse units such as dialogue utterances and even paragraphs or documents. As a result, these models have found applications in various NLP tasks, for example paraphrase detection; sentiment analysis; dialogue act tagging; machine translation; textual entailment; and so on, in many cases presenting state-of-the-art performance.

Being the natural evolution of the traditional and well-studied distributional models at the word level, CDMs are steadily evolving to a popular and active area of NLP. The topic has inspired a number of workshops and tutorials in top CL conferences such as ACL and EMNLP, special issues at high-profile journals, and it attracts a substantial amount of submissions in annual NLP conferences. The approaches employed by CDMs are as much as diverse as statistical machine leaning (Baroni and Zamparelli, 2010), linear algebra (Mitchell and Lapata, 2010), simple category theory (Coecke et al., 2010), or complex deep learning architectures based on neural networks and borrowing ideas from image processing (Socher et al., 2012; Kalchbrenner et al., 2014; Cheng and Kartsaklis, 2015). Furthermore, they create opportunities for interesting novel research, related for example to efficient methods for creating tensors for relational words such as verbs and adjectives (Grefenstette and Sadrzadeh, 2011), the treatment of logical and functional words in a distributional setting (Sadrzadeh et al., 2013; Sadrzadeh et al., 2014), or the role of polysemy and the way it affects composition (Kartsaklis and Sadrzadeh, 2013; Cheng and Kartsaklis, 2015). The purpose of this tutorial is to provide a concise introduction to this emerging field, presenting the different classes of CDMs and the various issues related to them in sufficient detail. The goal is to allow the student to understand the general philosophy of each approach, as well as its advantages and limitations with regard to the other alternatives.

2 Some background on CDMs

The purpose of a compositional distributional model is to provide a function that produces a vectorial representation of the meaning of a phrase or a sentence from the distributional vectors of the words therein. One can broadly classify such compositional distributional models to three categories:

Proceedings of COLING 2016, the 26th International Conference on Computational Linguistics: Tutorial Abstracts, pages 1–4, Osaka, Japan, December 11-17 2016.

- **Vector mixture models:** These are based on simple element-wise operations between vectors, such as addition and multiplication (Mitchell and Lapata, 2008). Vector mixture models constitute the simplest compositional method in distributional semantics. Despite their simplicity, though, have been proved a very hard-to-beat baseline for many of the more sophisticated models.

- **Tensor-based models:** In these models, relational words such as verbs and adjectives are tensors and matrices contracting and multiplying with noun (and noun-phrase) vectors (Coecke et al., 2010; Baroni and Zamparelli, 2010). Tensor-based models provide a solution to the problems of vector mixtures: they are not bag-of-words approaches and they respect the type-logical identities of special words, following an approach very much aligned with the formal semantics perspective. In fact, tensor-based composition is considered as the most linguistically motivated approach in compositional distributional semantics.

- **Neural-netword based models:** Models in which the compositional operator is part of a neural network and is usually optimized against a specific objective (Socher et al., 2012; Kalchbrenner et al., 2014; Cheng and Kartsaklis, 2015). Architectures that are usually employed are that of recursive or recurrent neural networks and convolutional neural networks. The non-linearity in combination with the layered approach in which neural networks are based make these models quite powerful, allowing them to simulate the behaviour of a range of functions much wider than the linear maps of tensor-based approaches.

Figure 1 provides an overview and a taxonomy of CDMs based on their theoretical power.

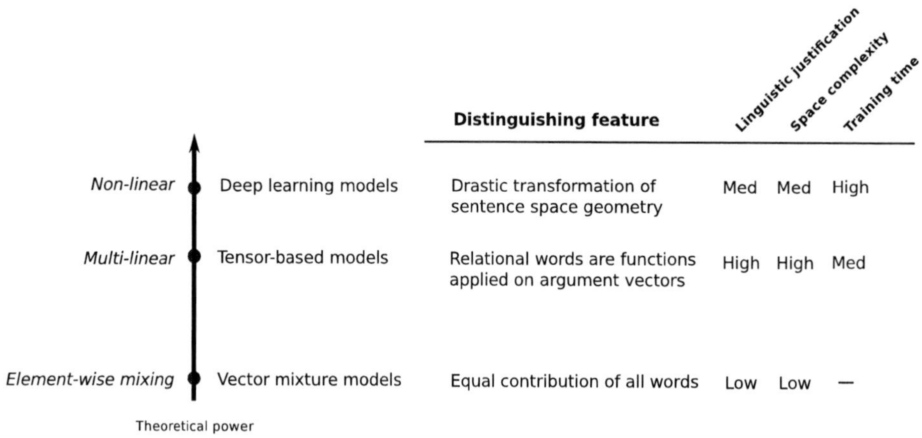

Figure 1: A hierarchy of compositional distributional models based on their theoretical power (Kartsaklis, 2015).

3 Outline

The tutorial aims at providing an introduction to these three classes of models, covering the most important aspects. Specifically, it will have the following structure (subject to time limitations):

- **Introduction.** The distributional hypothesis – Vector space models – The necessity for compositionality – Applications – An overview of CDMs

- **Vector mixture models.** Additive and multiplicative models – Interpretation – Practical applications

- **Tensor-based models.** Unifying grammar and semantics – Relational words as multi-linear maps – Extensions of the model

- **Machine learning/Deep learning models.** Introduction to NNs – Recursive and Recurrent NNs for composition – Connection to image processing – Convolutional NNs

- **Advanced issues and conclusion.** Logical and functional words – Lexical ambiguity and composition – Moving to discourse level – Concluding remarks

4 Prerequisites

The only prerequisite for attending the tutorial will be a knowledge of standard linear algebra, specifically with regard to vectors and their operations, vector spaces, matrices and linear maps. No special knowledge on advanced topics, such as category theory or neural networks, will be necessary.

5 Instructors

Mehrnoosh Sadrzadeh has taught undergraduate/graduate courses on logics of information from 2009-2012 in Oxford and in the Sino-European Winter School in Logic Language Computation in 2010 in China. She has experience in tutoring advance courses in logic for Oxford colleges. Since 2013, she teaches a course on computability in Queen Mary University London. She has long term experience in organising departmental and group research seminars in Oxford and Queen Mary and has experience in organising interdisciplinary workshops and conferences including the 11th International Conference on Computational Semantics (IWCS) and its satellite workshop Advances in Distributional Semantics in 2014. Her papers (Coecke et al., 2010; Grefenstette and Sadrzadeh, 2011) on compositional distributional semantics are among the highly cited papers of the field.

Dimitri Kartsaklis has been tutoring in various NLP and CS courses at the University of Oxford from 2012 to 2015. Recently he organized the 2016 Workshop on Semantic Spaces at the Intersection of NLP, Physics and Cognitive Science (with Martha Lewis and Laura Rimell). His work, focused on both theoretical and experimental aspects of compositional distributional models of meaning (for example, (Kartsaklis et al., 2012; Cheng and Kartsaklis, 2015)) has been published in various top-tier NLP and Computer Science conferences and journals.

6 Recommended reading

- Baroni and Zamparelli (2010). *Nouns are Vectors, Adjectives are Matrices: Representing adjective-noun constructions in semantic space*

- Coecke et al. (2010). *Mathematical Foundations for a Compositional Distributional Model of Meaning*

- Kartsaklis et al. (2012) *A Unified Sentence for Categorical Compositional Distributional Semantics: Theory and Experiments*

- Mitchell and Lapata (2010). *Composition in Distributional Models of Semantics*

- Socher et al. (2012). *Semantic Compositionality through Recursive Matrix-Vector Spaces*

- Turney and Pantel (2010). *From frequency to meaning: Vector space models of semantics*

References

M. Baroni and R. Zamparelli. 2010. Nouns are Vectors, Adjectives are Matrices. In *Proceedings of Conference on Empirical Methods in Natural Language Processing (EMNLP)*.

Jianpeng Cheng and Dimitri Kartsaklis. 2015. Syntax-aware multi-sense word embeddings for deep compositional models of meaning. In *Proceedings of the 2015 Conference on Empirical Methods in Natural Language Processing*, pages 1531–1542, Lisbon, Portugal, September. Association for Computational Linguistics.

B. Coecke, M. Sadrzadeh, and S. Clark. 2010. Mathematical Foundations for a Compositional Distributional Model of Meaning. Lambek Festschrift. *Linguistic Analysis*, 36:345–384.

Edward Grefenstette and Mehrnoosh Sadrzadeh. 2011. Experimental support for a categorical compositional distributional model of meaning. In *Proceedings of the 2011 Conference on Empirical Methods in Natural Language Processing*, pages 1394–1404, Edinburgh, Scotland, UK., July. Association for Computational Linguistics.

Nal Kalchbrenner, Edward Grefenstette, and Phil Blunsom. 2014. A convolutional neural network for modelling sentences. In *Proceedings of the 52nd Annual Meeting of the Association for Computational Linguistics (Volume 1: Long Papers)*, pages 655–665, Baltimore, Maryland, June. Association for Computational Linguistics.

Dimitri Kartsaklis and Mehrnoosh Sadrzadeh. 2013. Prior disambiguation of word tensors for constructing sentence vectors. In *Proceedings of the 2013 Conference on Empirical Methods in Natural Language Processing*, pages 1590–1601, Seattle, Washington, USA, October. Association for Computational Linguistics.

Dimitri Kartsaklis, Mehrnoosh Sadrzadeh, and Stephen Pulman. 2012. A unified sentence space for categorical distributional-compositional semantics: Theory and experiments. In *Proceedings of 24th International Conference on Computational Linguistics (COLING 2012): Posters*, pages 549–558, Mumbai, India, December. The COLING 2012 Organizing Committee.

Dimitri Kartsaklis. 2015. *Compositional Distributional Semantics with Compact Closed Categories and Frobenius Algebras*. Ph.D. thesis, University of Oxford.

J. Mitchell and M. Lapata. 2008. Vector-based Models of Semantic Composition. In *Proceedings of the 46th Annual Meeting of the Association for Computational Linguistics*, pages 236–244.

Jeff Mitchell and Mirella Lapata. 2010. Composition in distributional models of semantics. *Cognitive Science*, 34(8):1388–1439.

M. Sadrzadeh, S. Clark, and B. Coecke. 2013. The Frobenius anatomy of word meanings I: subject and object relative pronouns. *Journal of Logic and Computation*, Advance Access, October.

M. Sadrzadeh, S. Clark, and B. Coecke. 2014. The Frobenius anatomy of word meanings II: Possessive relative pronouns. *Journal of Logic and Computation*, June.

R. Socher, B. Huval, C. Manning, and Ng. A. 2012. Semantic compositionality through recursive matrix-vector spaces. In *Conference on Empirical Methods in Natural Language Processing 2012*.

Peter D Turney and Patrick Pantel. 2010. From frequency to meaning: Vector space models of semantics. *Journal of artificial intelligence research*, 37(1):141–188.

Chinese Textual Sentiment Analysis: Datasets, Resources and Tools

Lun-Wei Ku
Institute of Information Science
Academia Sinica
128 Academia Road, Section 2
Nankang, Taipei 11529, Taiwan
lwku@iis.sinica.edu.tw

Wei-Fan Chen
Institute of Information Science
Academia Sinica
128 Academia Road, Section 2
Nankang, Taipei 11529, Taiwan
viericwf@iis.sinica.edu.tw

1 Description

The rapid accumulation of data in social media (in million and billion scales) has imposed great challenges in information extraction, knowledge discovery, and data mining, and texts bearing sentiment and opinions are one of the major categories of user generated data in social media. Sentiment analysis is the main technology to quickly capture what people think from these text data, and is a research direction with immediate practical value in big data era. Learning such techniques will allow data miners to perform advanced mining tasks considering real sentiment and opinions expressed by users in additional to the statistics calculated from the physical actions (such as viewing or purchasing records) user perform, which facilitates the development of real-world applications. However, the situation that most tools are limited to the English language might stop academic or industrial people from doing research or products which cover a wider scope of data, retrieving information from people who speak different languages, or developing applications for worldwide users.

More specifically, sentiment analysis determines the polarities and strength of the sentiment-bearing expressions, and it has been an important and attractive research area. In the past decade, resources and tools have been developed for sentiment analysis in order to provide subsequent vital applications, such as product reviews, reputation management, call center robots, automatic public survey, etc. However, most of these resources are for the English language. Being the key to the understanding of business and government issues, sentiment analysis resources and tools are required for other major languages, e.g., Chinese.

In this tutorial, audience can learn the skills for retrieving sentiment from texts in another major language, Chinese, to overcome this obstacle. The goal of this tutorial is to introduce the proposed sentiment analysis technologies and datasets in the literature, and give the audience the opportunities to use resources and tools to process Chinese texts from the very basic preprocessing, i.e., word segmentation and part of speech tagging, to sentiment analysis, i.e., applying sentiment dictionaries and obtaining sentiment scores, through step-by-step instructions and a hand-on practice. The basic processing tools are from CKIP Participants can download these resources, use them and solve the problems they encounter in this tutorial.

This tutorial will begin from some background knowledge of sentiment analysis, such as how sentiment are categorized, where to find available corpora and which models are commonly applied, especially for the Chinese language. Then a set of basic Chinese text processing tools for word segmentation, tagging and parsing will be introduced for the preparation of mining sentiment and opinions. After bringing the idea of how to pre-process the Chinese language to the audience, I will describe our work on compositional Chinese sentiment analysis from words to sentences, and an application on social media text (Facebook) as an example. All our involved and recently developed related resources, including Chinese Morphological Dataset, Augmented NTU Sentiment Dictionary (ANTUSD), E-hownet with sentiment information, Chinese Opinion Treebank, and the CopeOpi Sentiment Scorer, will also be introduced and distributed in this tutorial. The tutorial will end by a hands-on session of how to use these materials and tools to process Chinese sentiment.

Proceedings of COLING 2016, the 26th International Conference on Computational Linguistics: Tutorial Abstracts, pages 5–8, Osaka, Japan, December 11-17 2016.

Tutorial Web Site: http://www.lunweiku.com/

2 Materials

Below is the summary of the materials that will be covered in this tutorial:

Resources: please see (Ku et al., 2011; Yohei et al., 2010; Ku et al., 2010; Ku et al., 2009; Ku et al., 2007; Ku et al., 2006; Wang and Ku, 2016; Chen and Ku, 2016; Chen et al., 2016).

Tools: please see (Chen et al., 2015; Ku et al., 2011; Ku et al., 2009; Ku and Chen, 2007).

3 Prerequisites

From which areas do we expect potential participants to come? Natural Language Processing, Web Mining, Machine Learning, Statistics, and Social Media Analytics

What prior knowledge, if any, do we expect from the audience? We do not require the audiences to have any background knowledge on the Chinese language. However, we expect the audience already understand some basic concepts and terminologies on natural language processing and sentiment analysis, such as part of speech tagging and opinion polarity.

What will the participants learn? The goal of this tutorial is to introduce the materials, resources and tool for Chinese sentiment Analysis. We will also highlight the main research challenges and unsolved issues in these areas, as there are still some room for improvement. Therefore, participants will not only acquire the knowledge and recent advances on Chinese sentiment analysis, but can also get ready for the basic Chinese text processing after this tutorial.

4 Lecturers

Lun-Wei Ku (lwku@iis.sinica.edu.tw) is now an Assistant Research Fellow in Institute of Information Science, Academia Sinica. She received her M.S. and Ph.D. degrees from Department of Computer Science and Information Engineering, National Taiwan University. Previously she worked as an assistant professor in the Department of Computer Science and Information Engineering, National Yunlin University of Science and Technology (Yuntech), Taiwan. Her research interests include natural language processing, information retrieval, and computational linguistics, especially on sentiment analysis. She has been working on Chinese sentiment analysis since year 2005 and was the co-organizer of NTCIR MOAT Task (Multilingual Opinion Analysis Task, traditional Chinese side) from year 2006 to 2010. Her international recognition includes CyberLink Technical Elite Fellowship (2007), IBM Ph.D. Fellowship (2008), ROCLING Doctorial Dissertation Distinction Award (2009), and Good Design Award Selected (2011). Other professional international activities she involved include: Member-at-Large, AFNLP (2016); Information Officier, ACM SIGHAN; Sentiment Analysis and Opinion Mining, Area Co-Chair, ACL-IJCNLP 2015 and EMNLP 2015; Publication Co-Chair, The 6th International Joint Conference on Natural Language Processing (IJCNLP 2013); Publicity Chair, The Twenty-fourth Conference on Computational Linguistics and Speech Processing (Rocling 2012); and Finance Chair, The Sixth Asia Information Retrieval Societies Conference (AIRS 2010).

Wei-Fan Chen (viericwf@iis.sinica.edu.tw) received the BS and MS degrees in communication engineering from National Chiao Tung University, in 2010 and 2012, respectively. He is a research assistant in the Institute of Information Science at Academia Sinica in Taipei, Taiwan. He has published papers in top, well recognized journals and conferences like IEEE TKDE (2016), COLING (2016), HCII (2015), AAAI symposium (2015), and ISCSLP (2012) and joined professional activities actively in NLP and AI domains. His research interests span a broad range of topics focusing on sentiment analysis, deep learning, computer-assisted language learning and speech processing.

5 Tentative Program

---

1. Overall Introduction (50 min)
Lecturer: Lun-Wei Ku

—-Definition, motivation, and challenge of the Chinese sentiment analysis
—-Introduction to related work and our previous results
—-Introduction to the Chinese language, mostly from the aspect of text processing

2. Introduction to the Resources and Tools (30 min)
Lecturer: Lun-Wei Ku

—-Available datasets
—-Available resources

Coffee Break: 20 min

---

3. Introduction to the Sentiment Analysis Tool: CopeOpi (20 min)
Lecturer: Lun-Wei Ku

4. The concept and design of CopeOpi Hands on: Real data (40 min)
Lecturer: Wei-Fan Chen

—-Getting data and environment ready
—-Preprocessing of the Chinese text: segmentation, par-of-speech tagging, parsing
—-Using NTUSD, ANTUSD and CopeOpi
—-Linking the sentiment and the lexical knowledge ontology

5. Final Wrap-up, Conclusion and Q/A (20 min)

Acknowledgements

Research of this paper was partially supported by Ministry of Science and Technology, Taiwan, under the contract MOST 104-2221-E-001-024-MY2.

References

Wei-Fan Chen and Lun-Wei Ku. 2016. UTCNN: a deep learning model of stance classification on social media text. In *COLING (to appear)*.

Wei-Fan Chen, Lun-Wei Ku, and Yann-Hui Lee. 2015. Mining supportive and unsupportive evidence from facebook using anti-reconstruction of the nuclear power plant as an example. In *Spring Symposium on Socio-Technical Behavior Mining: From Data to Decisions (2015 AAAI Symposium Series)*, pages 10–15.

Wei-Fan Chen, Fang-Yu Lin, and Lun-Wei Ku. 2016. WordForce: Visualizing controversial words in debates. In *COLING (to appear)*.

Lun-Wei Ku and Hsin-Hsi Chen. 2007. Mining opinions from the web: Beyond relevance retrieval. *Journal of the American Society for Information Science and Technology*, 58(12):1838–1850.

Lun-Wei Ku, Yu-Ting Liang, and Hsin-Hsi Chen. 2006. Opinion extraction, summarization and tracking in news and blog corpora. In *Proceedings of AAAI-2006 Spring Symposium on Computational Approaches to Analyzing Weblogs, AAAI Technical Report SS-06-03*, pages 100–107.

Lun-Wei Ku, Yong-Shen Lo, and Hsin-Hsi Chen. 2007. Test collection selection and gold standard generation for a multiply-annotated opinion corpus. In *Proceedings of 45th Annual Meeting of Association for Computational Linguistics (ACL)*, pages 89–92. Association for Computational Linguistics.

Lun-Wei Ku, Ting-Hao Huang, and Hsin-Hsi Chen. 2009. Using morphological and syntactic structures for chinese opinion analysis. In *Proceedings of Conference on Empirical Methods in Natural Language Processing (EMNLP)*, pages 1260–1269. Association for Computational Linguistics.

Lun-Wei Ku, Ting-Hao (Kenneth) Huang, and Hsin-Hsi Chen. 2010. Construction of chinese opinion treebank. In *Proceedings of the Seventh International Conference on Language Resources and Evaluation (LREC)*, pages 1315–1319.

Lun-Wei Ku, Ting-Hao (Kenneth) Huang, and Hsin-Hsi Chen. 2011. Predicting opinion dependency relations for opinion analysis. In *Proceedings of the 5th International Joint Conference on Natural Language Processing (IJCNLP)*, pages 345–353.

Shih-Ming Wang and Lun-Wei Ku. 2016. ANTUSD: A large chinese sentiment dictionary.

Seki Yohei, Ku Lun-Wei, Sun Le, Chen Hsin-Hsi, and Kando Noriko. 2010. Overview of multilingual opinion analysis task at ntcir-8-a step toward cross lingual opinion analysis. In *Proceedings of the 8th NTCIR Workshop Meeting on Evaluation of Information Access Technologies: Information Retrieval, Question Answering, and Cross-Lingual Information Access (NTCIR)*, pages 209–220.

Natural Language Processing for Intelligent Access to Scientific Information

Horacio Saggion and **Francesco Ronzano**
DTIC
Universitat Pompeu Fabra
Carrer Tanger 122, Barcelona (08018), Barcelona, Spain
{name.surname}@upf.edu

Abstract

During the last decade the amount of scientific information available on-line increased at an unprecedented rate. As a consequence, nowadays researchers are overwhelmed by an enormous and continuously growing number of articles to consider when they perform research activities like the exploration of advances in specific topics, peer reviewing, writing and evaluation of proposals. Natural Language Processing Technology represents a key enabling factor in providing scientists with intelligent patterns to access to scientific information. Extracting information from scientific papers, for example, can contribute to the development of rich scientific knowledge bases which can be leveraged to support intelligent knowledge access and question answering. Summarization techniques can reduce the size of long papers to their essential content or automatically generate state-of-the-art-reviews. Paraphrase or textual entailment techniques can contribute to the identification of relations across different scientific textual sources. This tutorial provides an overview of the most relevant tasks related to the processing of scientific documents, including but not limited to the in-depth analysis of the structure of the scientific articles, their semantic interpretation, content extraction and summarization.

1 Introduction

During the last decade the amount of scientific information available on-line increased at an unprecedented rate. Recent estimates reported that a new paper is published every 20 seconds (Munroe, 2013). PubMed includes more than 26M papers with a growth rate of about 1,370 new articles per day. Elsevier Scopus and Thomson Reuthers ISI Web of Knowledge respectively index more than 57 and 90 million papers. The Cornell University Library arXiv initiative provides access to over 1M e-prints from various scientific domains. At the same time, more and more papers can be freely read on-line since they are published as Open Access content (Björk et al., 2014): the full text of 27% of PubMed publications and more than 17% of the articles indexed by Scopus and ISI Web of Knowledge is available on-line for free and this percentages are considerably growing. The Directory of Open Access Journals, one of the most authoritative indexes of high quality, Open Access, peer-reviewed publications, lists more than 9,200 journals and 2.3M papers. Sometimes between 2017 and 2021, more than half of the global papers are expected to be published as Open Access content (Lewis, 2012). Moreover, several top conferences are making their articles freely available through dedicated archives even before the conference takes place. Social networks are by no means outside of this picture (Bar-Ilan et al., 2012; Thelwall et al., 2013): research networks like ResearchGate, Academia.edu or Mendeley are rapidly expanding, facilitating scientific information sharing (Haustein et al., 2014).

In this scenario of scientific information overload, **researchers, as well as any other interested actor, are overwhelmed by an enormous and continuously growing number of articles to consider**. Understanding recent advances in specific research fields, new methods and techniques, peer reviewing, writing and evaluation of research proposals and, in general, any activity that requires a careful and comprehensive assessment of scientific literature has turned into an extremely complex and time-consuming task for scientists world-wide.

Proceedings of COLING 2016, the 26th International Conference on Computational Linguistics: Tutorial Abstracts, pages 9–13, Osaka, Japan, December 11-17 2016.

In this context, **the Natural Language Processing community plays a central role in investigating and improving new approaches to the analysis of scientific information, thus uncovering incredible opportunities for contributions and experimentations**. The extraction and integration of information from scientific papers (Lipinski et al., 2013; Guo et al., 2011; Ronzano and Saggion, 2016b) constitute a key factor for the development of rich scientific knowledge bases which can be leveraged to support structured and semantically-enabled searches, intelligent question answering and personalized content recommendation (He et al., 2010; Huang et al., 2012). Summarization techniques can help to identify the essential contents of publications thus generating automatic state of the art reviews while paraphrase or textual entailment can contribute to identify relations across different scientific textual sources (Teufel and Moens, 2002; Abu-Jbara and Radev, 2011; Ronzano and Saggion, 2016a; Saggion and Lapalme, 2002; Saggion, 2008).

The objective of this tutorial is to provide a comprehensive overview of the most relevant problems we have to face when we mine scientific literature by means of Natural Language Processing Technologies, thus identifying challenges, solutions, and opportunities for our community. In particular, we consider approaches and tools useful to analyze and characterize a wide range of structural and semantic peculiarities of scientific articles, including document formats (Constantin et al., 2013; Lopez, 2009), layout-dependent information (Ramakrishnan et al., 2012; Luong et al., 2012; Councill et al., 2008), discursive structure (Liakata et al., 2010; Teufel et al., 2009; Fisas et al., 2015) and networks of citations (Teufel et al., 2006; Athar, 2011; Abu-Jbara et al., 2013). We discuss relevant scenarios where the availability of structured, semantically-annotated publications improves the way we benefit from scientific literature, including article summarization, scientific content search, selection and aggregation, and publication impact assessment. Related tools, applications, datasets and publication venues are also reviewed.

2 Outline

The half-day tutorial will review the following nine of top-level topics. For each topic, some of the core themes to discuss is specified.

1. **Scientific Information Overload: Challenges and Opportunities**
   - Overwhelmed by scientific publications (research articles, patents, tutorials, presentations, etc.)
   - Challenges & opportunities of scientific information overload
2. **Analyzing the Structure of Scientific Publications**
   - Available formats & contents
   - Retrieving textual contents from PDF publications
   - Document structure analysis
   - Patent analysis
3. **Mining the Semantics of Scientific Publications**
   - Text organization
   - Rhetorical structure analysis
   - Citation networks
   - Interpretation of citation purpose and polarity
4. **Extracting Information from Scientific Literature**
   - Scientific entities and their identification (names, formulas, numbers, drugs, genes, etc.)
   - Relation extraction problems (interactions, causal relations)
5. **Summarizing Scientific Information**

- Classic summarization approaches to scientific document
- Classification-based approaches
- Citation-based approaches
- Summarizing patents

6. **Language Resources for Scientific Text Analysis and Representation**
    - Available scientific corpora for experimentation
    - Lexical Resources in specialized domains
    - Ontologies for scientific information modelling

7. **Social Media and Science: new Opportunities**
    - Socially connected scientific entities
    - Social Media metrics to assess research impact

8. **Applications, Challenges and Projects**
    - Scientific literature on-line portals
    - Discussion venues and challenges
    - Relevant projects

9. **Mining scientific articles with the Dr. Inventor Framework**
    - The Dr. Inventor project
    - Overview and demo of the Dr. Inventor Scientific Text Mining Framework

3 Tutorial Web Site

More details on this tutorial can be accessed on-line at: http://taln.upf.edu/pages/coling2016tutorial/.

4 Organizers

Horacio Saggion holds a PhD in Computer Science from Universite de Montreal, Canada. He obtained his BSc in Computer Science from Universidad de Buenos Aires in Argentina, and his MSc in Computer Science from UNICAMP in Brazil. Horacio is an Associate Professor at the Department of Information and Communication Technologies, Universitat Pompeu Fabra (UPF), Barcelona. He is a member of the Natural Language Processing group where he works on automatic text summarization, text simplification, information extraction, sentiment analysis and related topics. His research is empirical combining symbolic, pattern-based approaches and statistical and machine learning techniques. Before joining Universitat Pompeu Fabra, he worked at the University of Sheffield for a number of UK and European research projects (SOCIS, MUMIS, MUSING, GATE, CUBREPORTER) developing competitive human language technology. He was also an invited researcher at John Hopkins University for a project on multilingual text summarization. He is currently principal investigator for UPF in several EU and national projects.

Horacio has published over 100 works in leading scientific journals, conferences, and books in the field of human language technology. He organized four international workshops in the areas of text summarization and information extraction and was co-chair of STIL 2009. He is co-editor of a book on multilingual, multisource information extraction and summarization published by Springer in 2013. Horacio is member of the ACL, IEEE, ACM, and SADIO. He is a regular programme committee member for international conferences such as ACL, EACL, COLING, EMNLP, IJCNLP, IJCAI and is an active reviewer for international journals in computer science, information processing, and human language technology. Horacio has given courses, tutorials, and invited talks at a number of international events including LREC, ESSLLI, IJCNLP, NLDB, and RuSSIR.

Francesco Ronzano holds a PhD in Information Engineering from the University of Pisa, Italy. Francesco is currently a Researcher of the Natural Language Processing Group (TALN) at the Department of Information and Communication Technologies, Universitat Pompeu Fabra, Barcelona, where he deals with machine learning approaches for information extraction and text summarization, with special focus on scientific publishing and social media analysis. Francesco has several years of research experience mainly in the context of National (Italian and Spanish) and European Research Projects related to the exploitation of machine learning approaches and Web technologies to foster Language Technologies. His research interests include on-line data semantics, machine learning, knowledge representation and Semantic Web applications. Francesco has coordinated the development of the Dr. Inventor Text Mining Framework, an software tool to mine a wide range of facets of scientific publications.

Francesco has contributed to more than 40 publications among book chapters, journal articles, conference papers. He acted as reviewer to international conferences including AAAI, EMNLP, LREC, RANLP, etc.

Acknowledgements

We acknowledge (partial) support by the Spanish Ministry of Economy and Competitiveness under the Maria de Maeztu Units of Excellence Programme (MDM-2015-0502) and the European Project Dr. Inventor (FP7-ICT-2013.8.1 - Grant no: 611383).

References

Amjad Abu-Jbara and Dragomir Radev. 2011. Coherent citation-based summarization of scientific papers. In *Proc. of 49th Annual Meeting of the ACL: Human Language Techologies*, pages 500–509. ACL, June.

Amjad Abu-Jbara, Jefferson Ezra, and Dragomir R Radev. 2013. Purpose and polarity of citation: Towards nlp-based bibliometrics. In *HLT-NAACL*, pages 596–606.

Awais Athar. 2011. Sentiment analysis of citations using sentence structure-based features. In *Proceedings of the ACL 2011 student session*, pages 81–87. Association for Computational Linguistics.

Judit Bar-Ilan, Stefanie Haustein, Isabella Peters, Jason Priem, Hadas Shema, and Jens Terliesner. 2012. Beyond citations: Scholars' visibility on the social web. *arXiv preprint arXiv:1205.5611*.

Bo-Christer Björk, Mikael Laakso, Patrik Welling, and Patrik Paetau. 2014. Anatomy of green open access. *Journal of the Association for Information Science and Technology*, 65(2):237–250.

Alexandru Constantin, Steve Pettifer, and Andrei Voronkov. 2013. Pdfx: fully-automated pdf-to-xml conversion of scientific literature. In *Proceedings of the 2013 ACM symposium on Document engineering*, pages 177–180. ACM.

Isaac G Councill, C Lee Giles, and Min-Yen Kan. 2008. Parscit: an open-source crf reference string parsing package. In *LREC*, volume 8, pages 661–667.

Beatriz Fisas, Francesco Ronzano, and Horacio Saggion. 2015. On the discoursive structure of computer graphics research papers. In *The 9th Linguistic Annotation Workshop held in conjuncion with NAACL 2015*, page 42.

Yufan Guo, Anna Korhonen, and Thierry Poibeau. 2011. A weakly-supervised approach to argumentative zoning of scientific documents. In *Proceedings of the Conference on Empirical Methods in Natural Language Processing*, pages 273–283. Association for Computational Linguistics.

Stefanie Haustein, Vincent Larivière, Mike Thelwall, Didier Amyot, and Isabella Peters. 2014. Tweets vs. mendeley readers: How do these two social media metrics differ? *IT-Information Technology*, 56(5):207–215.

Qi He, Jian Pei, Daniel Kifer, Prasenjit Mitra, and Lee Giles. 2010. Context-aware citation recommendation. In *Proceedings of the 19th international conference on World wide web*, pages 421–430. ACM.

Wenyi Huang, Saurabh Kataria, Cornelia Caragea, Prasenjit Mitra, C Lee Giles, and Lior Rokach. 2012. Recommending citations: translating papers into references. In *Proceedings of the 21st ACM international conference on Information and knowledge management*, pages 1910–1914. ACM.

David W Lewis. 2012. The inevitability of open access. *College & Research Libraries*, 73(5):493–506.

Maria Liakata, Simone Teufel, Advaith Siddharthan, Colin R Batchelor, et al. 2010. Corpora for the conceptualisation and zoning of scientific papers. In *LREC*.

Mario Lipinski, Kevin Yao, Corinna Breitinger, Joeran Beel, and Bela Gipp. 2013. Evaluation of header metadata extraction approaches and tools for scientific pdf documents. In *Proceedings of the 13th ACM/IEEE-CS joint conference on Digital libraries*, pages 385–386. ACM.

Patrice Lopez. 2009. Grobid: Combining automatic bibliographic data recognition and term extraction for scholarship publications. In *International Conference on Theory and Practice of Digital Libraries*, pages 473–474. Springer.

Minh-Thang Luong, Thuy Dung Nguyen, and Min-Yen Kan. 2012. Logical structure recovery in scholarly articles with rich document features. *Multimedia Storage and Retrieval Innovations for Digital Library Systems*, 270.

Randall Munroe. 2013. The rise of open access. *Science*, 342(6154):58–59.

Cartic Ramakrishnan, Abhishek Patnia, Eduard Hovy, and Gully APC Burns. 2012. Layout-aware text extraction from full-text pdf of scientific articles. *Source code for biology and medicine*, 7(1):1.

Francesco Ronzano and Horacio Saggion. 2016a. An empirical assessment of citation information in scientific summarization. In *International Conference on Applications of Natural Language to Information Systems*, pages 318–325. Springer.

Francesco Ronzano and Horacio Saggion. 2016b. Knowledge extraction and modeling from scientific publications. *Proceedings of the Semantics, Analytics, Visualisation: Enhancing Scholarly Data Workshop*.

Horacio Saggion and Guy Lapalme. 2002. Generating indicative-informative summaries with sumum. *Comput. Linguist.*, 28(4):497–526, December.

Horacio Saggion. 2008. SUMMA: A Robust and Adaptable Summarization Tool. *Traitement Automatique des Langues*, 49(2):103–125.

Simone Teufel and Marc Moens. 2002. Summarizing scientific articles: experiments with relevance and rhetorical status. *Computational linguistics*, 28(4):409–445.

Simone Teufel, Advaith Siddharthan, and Dan Tidhar. 2006. Automatic classification of citation function. In *Proceedings of the 2006 conference on empirical methods in natural language processing*, pages 103–110. Association for Computational Linguistics.

Simone Teufel, Advaith Siddharthan, and Colin Batchelor. 2009. Towards discipline-independent argumentative zoning: evidence from chemistry and computational linguistics. In *Proceedings of the 2009 Conference on Empirical Methods in Natural Language Processing: Volume 3-Volume 3*, pages 1493–1502. Association for Computational Linguistics.

Mike Thelwall, Stefanie Haustein, Vincent Larivière, and Cassidy R Sugimoto. 2013. Do altmetrics work? twitter and ten other social web services. *PloS one*, 8(5):e64841.

Quality Estimation for Language Output Applications

Carolina Scarton and **Gustavo Henrique Paetzold** and **Lucia Specia**
Department of Computer Science
University of Sheffield, UK
{c.scarton,g.h.paetzold,l.specia}@sheffield.ac.uk

Description

Quality Estimation (QE) is the task of predicting the quality of the output of Natural Language Processing (NLP) applications without relying on human references. This is a very appealing method for language output applications, i.e. applications that take as input a text and produce a different text as output, for example, Machine Translation, Text Summarisation and Text Simplification. For these applications, producing human references is time consuming and expensive. More important, QE enables quality assessments of the output of these applications *on the fly*, making it possible for users to decide whether or not they can rely and use the texts produced. This would not be possible with evaluation methods that require datasets with gold standard annotations. Finally, QE can predict scores that reflect how good an output is for a given purpose and, therefore, is considered a task-based evaluation method. The only requirement for QE are data points with quality scores to train supervised machine learning models, which can then be used to predict quality scores for any number of unseen data points. The main challenges for such a task rely on devising effective features and appropriate labels for quality at different granularity levels (words, sentences, documents, etc.). Sophisticated machine learning techniques, such as multi-task learning to model biases and preferences of annotators, can also contribute to making the models more reliable.

Figure 1 illustrates a standard framework for QE during its training stage. Features for training the QE model are extracted from both source (original) and target (output) texts (and optionally from the system that produced the output). A QE model can be trained to predict the quality at different granularity levels (such as words, sentences and documents) and also for different purposes. Therefore the input text, the features, the labels and the machine learning algorithm will depend on the specificities of the task variant. For example, if the task is to predict the quality of machine translated sentences for post-editing purposes, a common quality label could be post-editing time (i.e. the time required for a human to fix the machine translation output), while features could include indicators related to the complexity of the source sentence and the fluency of the target sentence.

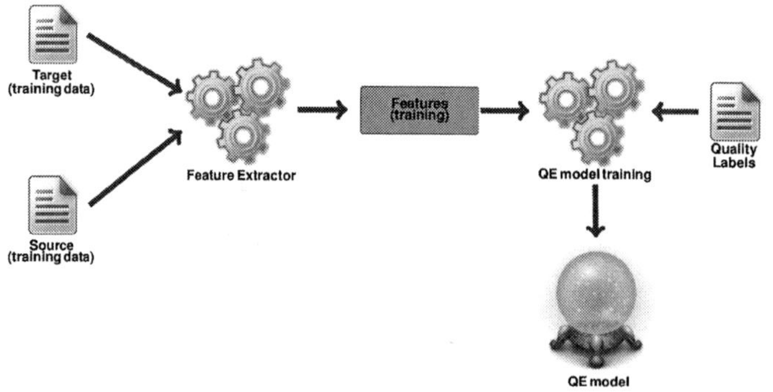

Figure 1: QE training framework.

Proceedings of COLING 2016, the 26th International Conference on Computational Linguistics: Tutorial Abstracts, pages 14–17, Osaka, Japan, December 11-17 2016.

Figure 2 illustrates the usage of a trained QE model. Unseen unlabelled data is the input for such a stage. The same features that were used to train the QE model are extracted from these instances and quality predictions are then produced by the model.

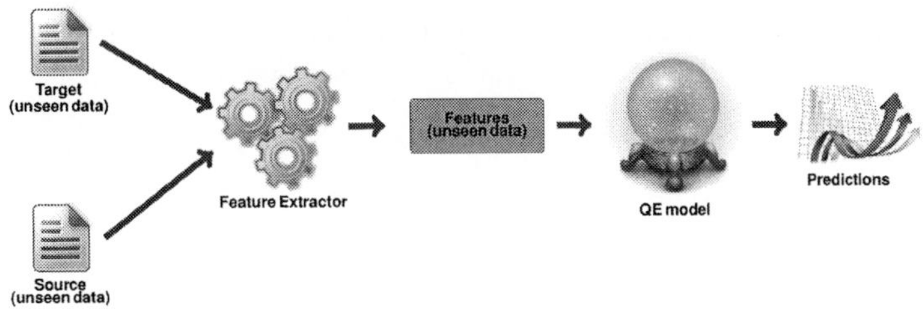

Figure 2: QE model prediction.

QE is a reasonably new field, but over the last decade has become particularly popular in the area of **Machine Translation (MT)**. With the goal of providing a prediction on the **quality of a machine translated text**, QE systems have the potential to make MT more useful in a number of scenarios, for example, improving post-editing efficiency by filtering out segments which would require more effort or time to correct than to translate from scratch (Specia, 2011), selecting high quality segments (Soricut and Echihabi, 2010), selecting a translation from either an MT system or a translation memory (He et al., 2010), selecting the best translation from multiple MT systems (Shah and Specia, 2014), and highlighting words or phrases that need revision (Bach et al., 2011).

Sentence-level QE represents the vast majority of existing work. It has been addressed as a supervised machine learning task using a variety of algorithms to train models from examples of sentence translations annotated with quality labels (e.g. 1 to 5 *likert* scores). This prediction level has been covered in shared tasks organised by the Workshop on Statistical Machine Translation (WMT) annually since 2012 (Callison-Burch et al., 2012; Bojar et al., 2013; Bojar et al., 2014; Bojar et al., 2015; Bojar et al., 2016). While standard algorithms can be used to build prediction models, key to this task is work of feature engineering.

Word-level QE has also been receiving significant attention. It is seemingly a more challenging task, where a quality label is to be produced for each target word. An additional challenge for this level is the acquisition of sizeable training sets. Significant efforts have been made (including four years of shared tasks at WMT), leading to an increase in interest in word-level QE over the years. An application that can benefit from word-level QE is spotting errors (incorrect words) in a post-editing/revision scenario. A recent variant of this task is quality prediction at the level of phrases (Logacheva and L.Specia, 2015; Blain et al., 2016), where a phrase can be defined in different ways, e.g. using the segmentation from a statistical MT decoder in WMT16 (Bojar et al., 2016).

Document-level QE has received much less attention than the other levels. This task consists in predicting a single quality label for an entire document, be it an absolute score (Scarton and Specia, 2014) or a relative ranking of translations by one or more MT systems (Soricut and Echihabi, 2010). It is most useful for *gisting* purposes, where post-editing is not an option. Two shared tasks on document-level QE were organised at WMT15 and WMT16. An open research question when it comes to document-level QE is to define effective quality labels for entire documents (Scarton et al., 2015).

A few QE frameworks have been proposed in the last couple of years, namely (Gonzàlez et al., 2012; Specia et al., 2013; Servan et al., 2015; Logacheva et al., 2016; Specia et al., 2015). QUEST++ (Specia et al., 2015)[1] is the most widely used one. It is a significantly refactored and expanded version of QUEST (Specia et al., 2013). It has been used as the official baseline system during all editions of the WMT shared task on QE (WMT12-WMT16) and is often the starting point upon which other participants build their systems, particularly for feature extraction. It has two main modules: feature extraction and

[1] `https://github.com/ghpaetzold/questplusplus`

machine learning. The feature extraction module can operate at sentence, word and document-level and includes the extraction of shallow and linguistic-motivated features. The machine learning module provides wrappers for various algorithms in SCIKIT-LEARN (Pedregosa et al., 2011), in addition to a few implementations of stand-alone algorithms such as Gaussian Processes for regression.

QE of MT will be the focus of this tutorial, but we will also introduce related work in applications such as Text Summarisation and discuss how the same framework could be applied or adapted to other language output applications.

Tutorial Structure

Theoretical aspects of QE (1h30) In the first part of this tutorial we will introduce the task of QE, show the standard framework for it and describe the three most common levels of prediction in QE for MT. We will also introduce various ways in which different kinds of Neural Networks can be employed in QE. Challenges and future work for each level will be discussed. We will cover related work for NLP applications other than MT, including ideas on how to adapt the current QE pipeline. In addition, examples of uses of QE in research and industry will be illustrated.

Hands-on QuEst++ (1h00) The second part of the tutorial will cover a hands-on QuEst++ activity, showing how to install and run it for examples available at all prediction levels. We will describe the two modules of this framework: feature extractor (implemented in Java) and machine learning (implemented in Python). We will guide participants to add an example of linguistic feature to QuEst++ using external resources, showing the interaction between classes and configuration files. We will also show how to write a wrapper for a new machine learning algorithm from SCIKIT-LEARN .

More information will be made available at the tutorial's website: `http://staffwww.dcs.shef.ac.uk/people/C.Scarton/qe-tutorial/`.

Instructors

Carolina Scarton is a PhD student and a Research Assistant at the University of Sheffield, UK, being supervised by Professor Lucia Specia. The topic of her thesis is on document-level assessment for QE of MT. More specifically, her research focuses on how to assess machine translated documents in order to build QE models at document level and the development of features for document-level QE (including the contribution on document-level QE for QuEst++). She has published several papers in international conferences in topics related to QE of MT and organised the document-level task on WMT15[2] and WMT16[3] QE shared tasks. Additionally, her research topics also include Readability Assessment, Text Simplification and Language Acquisition. Carolina received a Master degree in Computer Science from the University of São Paulo, Brazil, in 2013.
webpage: `http://www.dcs.shef.ac.uk/people/C.Scarton/`

Gustavo Henrique Paetzold is a Research Assistant at the University of Sheffield, UK, with a Ph.D. in Computational Linguistics. His main areas of expertise are Text Adaptation and Quality Estimation. Throughout the past few years, Gustavo has published several contributions to QE in international conferences, and is one of the main contributors to the QuEst++ framework, which will be feature in this tutorial. He has also experience in developing QE solutions for industry, given his brief collaboration with Iconic Translation Machines Ltd.
webpage: `https://gustavopaetzold.wordpress.com`

Lucia Specia is a Professor of Language Engineering and a member of the Natural Language Processing group at the University of Sheffield, UK. Her main areas of research are MT, Text Adaptation, and Quality Evaluation and Estimation of language output applications. Prof Specia is the recipient of an ERC Starting Grant on Multimodal Machine Translation (2016-2021) and is currently involved in various other funded research projects, including the European initiatives QT21 (Quality Translation 21) and

[2]`http://www.statmt.org/wmt15/quality-estimation-task.html`
[3]`http://www.statmt.org/wmt16/quality-estimation-task.html`

Cracker (Cracking the Language Barrier). She has published over 100 research papers in peer-reviewed journals and conference proceedings and organised a number of workshops in the area of NLP. She has given six tutorials on topics related to MT.
webpage: `www.dcs.shef.ac.uk/people/L.Specia/`

References

N. Bach, F. Huang, and Y. Al-Onaizan. 2011. Goodness: a method for measuring MT confidence. In *ACL11*.

F. Blain, V. Logacheva, and L. Specia. 2016. Phrase level segmentation and labelling of machine translation errors. In *LREC16*.

O. Bojar, C. Buck, C. Callison-Burch, C. Federmann, B. Haddow, P. Koehn, C. Monz, M. Post, R. Soricut, and L. Specia. 2013. Findings of the 2013 Workshop on SMT. In *WMT13*.

O. Bojar, C. Buck, C. Federmann, B. Haddow, P. Koehn, J. Leveling, C. Monz, P. Pecina, M. Post, H. Saint-Amand, R. Soricut, L. Specia, and A. Tamchyna. 2014. Findings of the 2014 Workshop on SMT. In *WMT14*.

O. Bojar, R. Chatterjee, C. Federmann, B. Haddow, M. Huck, C. Hockamp, P. Koehn, V. Logacheva, C. Monz, M. Negri, M. Post, C. Scarton, L. Specia, and M. Turchi. 2015. Findings of the 2015 Workshop on SMT. In *WMT15*.

O. Bojar, R. Chatterjee, C. Federmann, Y. Graham, B. Haddow, M. Huck, A. Jimeno Yepes, P. Koehn, V. Logacheva, C. Monz, M. Negri, A. Neveol, M. Neves, M. Popel, M. Post, R. Rubino, C. Scarton, L. Specia, M. Turchi, K. Verspoor, and M. Zampieri. 2016. Findings of the 2016 Conference on Machine Translation. In *WMT16*.

C. Callison-Burch, P. Koehn, C. Monz, M. Post, R. Soricut, and L. Specia. 2012. Findings of the 2012 Workshop on SMT. In *WMT12*.

M. Gonzàlez, J. Giménez, and L. Màrquez. 2012. A Graphical Interface for MT Evaluation and Error Analysis. In *ACL12*.

Y. He, Y. Ma, J. van Genabith, and A. Way. 2010. Bridging SMT and TM with translation recommendation. In *ACL10*.

V. Logacheva and L.Specia. 2015. Phrase-level quality estimation for machine translation. In *IWSLT15*.

V. Logacheva, C. Hokamp, and L. Specia. 2016. Marmot: A toolkit for translation quality estimation at the word level. In *LREC16*.

F. Pedregosa, G. Varoquaux, A. Gramfort, V. Michel, B. Thirion, O. Grisel, M. Blondel, P. Prettenhofer, R. Weiss, V. Dubourg, J. Vanderplas, A. Passos, D. Cournapeau, M. Brucher, M. Perrot, and E. Duchesnay. 2011. Scikit-learn: Machine learning in Python. *Journal of Machine Learning Research*, 12.

C. Scarton and L. Specia. 2014. Document-level translation quality estimation: exploring discourse and pseudo-references. In *EAMT14*.

C. Scarton, M. Zampieri, M. Vela, J. van Genabith, and L. Specia. 2015. Searching for Context: a Study on Document-Level Labels for Translation Quality Estimation. In *EAMT15*.

C. Servan, N.-T. Le, N. Q. Luong, B. Lecouteux, and L. Besacier. 2015. An Open Source Toolkit for Word-level Confidence Estimation in Machine Translation. In *IWSLT15*.

K. Shah and L. Specia. 2014. Quality estimation for translation selection. In *EAMT14*.

R. Soricut and A. Echihabi. 2010. Trustrank: Inducing trust in automatic translations via ranking. In *ACL10*.

L. Specia, K. Shah, J. G. C. de Souza, and T. Cohn. 2013. Quest - a translation quality estimation framework. In *ACL13*.

L. Specia, G. H. Paetzold, and C. Scarton. 2015. Multi-level Translation Quality Prediction with QuEst++. In *ACL-IJCNLP15 - System Demonstrations*.

L. Specia. 2011. Exploiting objective annotations for measuring translation post-editing effort. In *EAMT11*.

Translationese: Between Human and Machine Translation

Shuly Wintner
Department of Computer Science, University of Haifa
Mount Carmel, Haifa, Israel
shuly@cs.haifa.ac.il
http://www.cs.haifa.ac.il/~shuly

Brief Description

Translated texts, in any language, have unique characteristics that set them apart from texts originally written in the same language. Translation Studies is a research field that focuses on investigating these characteristics. Until recently, research in machine translation (MT) has been entirely divorced from translation studies. The main goal of this tutorial is to introduce some of the findings of translation studies to researchers interested mainly in machine translation, and to demonstrate that awareness to these findings can result in better, more accurate MT systems.

First, we will survey some theoretical hypotheses of translation studies. Focusing on the unique properties of *translationese* (the sub-language of translated texts), we will distinguish between properties resulting from *interference* from the source language (the so-called "fingerprints" of the source language on the translation product) and properties that are source-language-independent, and that are presumably universal. The latter include phenomena resulting from three main processes: *simplification*, *standardization* and *explicitation*. All these phenomena will be defined, explained and exemplified.

Then, we will describe several works that use standard (supervised and unsupervised) text classification techniques to distinguish between translations and originals, in several languages. We will focus on the features that best separate between the two classes, and how these features corroborate some (but not all) of the hypotheses set forth by translation studies scholars.

Next, we will discuss several computational works that show that awareness to translationese can improve machine translation. Specifically, we will show that language models compiled from translated texts are more fitting to the reference sets than language models compiled from originals. We will also show that translation models compiled from texts that were (manually) translated from the source to the target are much better than translation models compiled from texts that were translated in the reverse direction. We will briefly discuss how translation models can be adapted to better reflect the properties of translationese.

Finally, we will touch upon some related issues and current research directions. For example, we will discuss recent work that addresses the identification of the source language from which target language texts were translated. We will show that native language identification (in particular, of language learners) is a closely related task to the identification of translationese. Time permitting, we will also discuss work aimed at distinguishing between native and (advanced, fluent) non-native speakers.

Outline

- Translation Studies hypotheses
  - Simplification
  - Explicitation
  - Normalization
  - Interference
- Identification of translationese
  - Text classification

Proceedings of COLING 2016, the 26th International Conference on Computational Linguistics: Tutorial Abstracts, pages 18–19, Osaka, Japan, December 11-17 2016.

  - Features
  - Supervised classification
  - Unsupervised classification

- Relevance for machine translation
  - Improving language models
  - Improving translation models

- Related issues
  - Identification of the source language of translations
  - Native language identification
  - Distinguishing between native and non-native speakers

Instructor

Shuly Wintner is a professor of computer science at the University of Haifa, Israel. His research spans various areas of computational linguistics and natural language processing, including formal grammars, morphology, syntax, language resources, and translation. He served as the editor-in-chief of Springer's Research on Language and Computation, a program co-chair of EACL-2006, and the general chair of EACL-2014. He was among the founders, and twice (6 years) the chair, of ACL SIG Semitic. Currently, he serves as the Head of the Department of Computer Science in Haifa. Shuly has an extensive teaching experience, including tutorials at EACL-2012, ICGI-2012, NAACL-2004, MT-Summit 2003 and COLING-2000; five ESSLLI courses; three courses at the International PhD School in Formal Languages and Applications; and two at the Erasmus Mundus Master course in Language and Communication Technology.

Succinct Data Structures for NLP-at-Scale

Matthias Petri and **Trevor Cohn**
Computing and Information Systems
The University of Melbourne, Australia
first.last@unimelb.edu.au

1 Motivation

Succinct data structures involve the use of novel data structures, compression technologies, and other mechanisms to allow data to be stored in extremely small memory or disk footprints, while still allowing for efficient access to the underlying data. They have successfully been applied in areas such as Information Retrieval and Bioinformatics to create highly compressible in-memory search indexes which provide efficient search functionality over datasets which traditionally could only be processed using external memory data structures.

Modern technologies in this space are not well known within the NLP community, but have the potential to revolutionise NLP, particularly the application to 'big data' in the form of terabyte and larger corpora. This tutorial will present a practical introduction to the most important succinct data structures, tools, and applications with the intent of providing the researchers with a jump-start into this domain. The focus of this tutorial will be efficient text processing utilising space efficient representations of suffix arrays, suffix trees and searchable integer compression schemes with specific applications of succinct data structures to common NLP tasks such as n-gram language modelling.

2 Tutorial Outline

The half-day tutorial contains several sessions, each with a practical component, on the following topics:

Introduction and Motivation (15 Minutes) In the first session we motivate the need for succinct structures. We discuss existing applications and examples in IR and NLP, and benefits of succinct structures when facing terabyte scale text processing problems.

Basic Technologies (20 Minutes) In the second session we give a brief introduction into the theoretical foundation of succinct data structures. We discuss the concept of bitvectors, data compression and basic RANK and SELECT on bitvectors which are at the core of most succinct data structures. Next we introduce several simple succinct structures such as a succinct tree representation (LOUDS) and variable size, constant access time, integer representations (DAC).

Index based Pattern Matching (20 Minutes) In the next session we start the tutorial by briefly revisiting several classical search indexes such as Suffix Arrays and Suffix Trees which can provide search functionality used in many NLP applications. We then introduce the notation of a Compressed Suffix Array (CSA), which substantially reduces the space requirement of a Suffix Array while providing the same functionality.

Compressed Suffix Arrays Internals: How does it all work (30 Minutes) This session covers the underlying technical principals of compressed suffix arrays. This includes concepts such as the Burrows-Wheeler Transform, backward search and wavelet trees.

Compressed Suffix Trees (CST): Concepts (10 Minutes) Here we extend the concept of compressed suffix arrays to compressed suffix trees (CST). This includes additional structures to represent the shape of the tree as well as additional operations supported by the CST which are important for several NLP applications.

Proceedings of COLING 2016, the 26th International Conference on Computational Linguistics: Tutorial Abstracts, pages 20–21, Osaka, Japan, December 11-17 2016.

Utilizing CSA and CST in the context of Language Models (20 Minutes) This session will cover our line of research on unlimited order language modelling with modified Kneser-Ney smoothing. Efficient methods for storing and querying language models are critical for scaling to large corpora and high Markov orders. At its core, our approach uses a compressed suffix tree of text which provides near optimal compression while supporting efficient search. We present algorithms for on-the-fly computation of probabilities under a Kneser-Ney and Modified Kneser-Ney language models. Our approach is exact and on par with leading language modelling toolkits in terms of speed while being several order of magnitudes smaller.

Other applications of Succinct Structures in NLP (10 Minutes) The last session briefly touch on advanced succinct structures consisting of Range Minimum / Maximum Queries, Succinct Tries, Treaps and 2D-range query structures.

3 Instructors

Matthias Petri is an expert in the field of practical succinct data structures and one of the main authors of the quasi-standard succinct data structure library (SDSL) used by many researchers in the field. He has several publications in top journals and conferences in algorithms, algorithm engineering and information retrieval (e.g., WWW, DCC, ALENEX, SIGIR, SPE, CPM). He specializes in algorithms engineering and applying succinct data structures to large scale text indexing problems and is currently employed as a Research Fellow working on text indexing and data compression at the University of Melbourne.

Trevor Cohn is an expert in statistical and probabilistic approaches to natural language processing, with a focus on models and algorithms for structured prediction. He publishes in the top journals and conferences in language processing and machine learning (ACL, EMNLP, AAAI). His work includes applications to parsing, translation, information extraction, summarisation and the modelling of social media. He is currently a Senior Lecturer and ARC Future Fellow at the University of Melbourne.

Acknowledgments

This tutorial was supported by the Australian Research Council (FT130101105) and a Google Faculty Research Award.

References

Stanley F Chen and Joshua Goodman. 1999. An empirical study of smoothing techniques for language modeling. *Computer Speech & Language*, 13(4):359–393.

Paolo Ferragina and Giovanni Manzini. 2000. Opportunistic data structures with applications. In *Proceedings of the Annual Symposium on Foundations of Computer Science*, pages 390–398.

Simon Gog, Timo Beller, Alistair Moffat, and Matthias Petri. 2014. From theory to practice: Plug and play with succinct data structures. In *Proceedings of the International Symposium on Experimental Algorithms*, pages 326–337.

Enno Ohlebusch, Johannes Fischer, and Simon Gog. 2010. CST++. In *Proceedings of the International Symposium on String Processing and Information Retrieval*, pages 322–333.

Ehsan Shareghi, Matthias Petri, Gholamreza Haffari, and Trevor Cohn. 2016. Fast, small and exact: Infinite-order language modelling with compressed suffix trees. *Transactions of the Association for Computational Linguistics*, 4:477–490.

Peter Weiner. 1973. Linear pattern matching algorithms. In *Proceedings of the Annual Symposium Switching and Automata Theory*, pages 1–11.

The Role of Wikipedia in Text Analysis and Retrieval

Marius Paşca
Google Inc.
Mountain View, California 94043
mars@google.com

1 Tutorial Description

It has long been recognized that access to world knowledge should be beneficial to understanding written language, whether for deciding how phrases in a particular sentence should be translated; what their senses are in a dictionary; what entities they refer to, and in what relations. The emergence of knowledge resources in machine-readable form enabled advances in a wide range of tasks related to text analysis and retrieval.

High expectations of quality and consistency in expert-created knowledge resources reduce the number of their potential contributors. In turn, this makes it difficult to maintain the resources; refresh or add knowledge of the same type, as it becomes relevant over time; or incorporate knowledge of a new type. Especially in the context of Web search, where queries in the long tail reflect different backgrounds and interests of millions of users, resources that are more likely to be stale or incomplete are less likely to consistently provide value. As a counterpart to expert-created resources, non-expert users may collaboratively create large resources of unstructured or semi-structured knowledge, a leading representative of which is Wikipedia. The decentralized construction leads to the inherent lack of any guarantees of quality or reliability, and cannot rule out attempts at adversarial content editing. Nevertheless, articles within Wikipedia are incrementally edited and improved. Collectively, they form an easily-editable collection, reflecting an ever-growing number of topics of interest to people, in general, and Web users, in particular. Furthermore, the conversion of semi-structured content from Wikipedia into structured data makes knowledge from Wikipedia or from one of its derivatives potentially even more suitable for use in text processing or information retrieval.

This tutorial examines the role of Wikipedia in tasks related to text analysis and retrieval. Text analysis tasks, which take advantage of Wikipedia, include coreference resolution, word sense and entity disambiguation, to name only a few. More prominently, they include information extraction. In information retrieval, a better understanding of the structure and meaning of queries enables a better match of queries against documents, and retrieval of knowledge panels for queries asking about popular entities. Concretely, the tutorial teaches the audience about characteristics, advantages and limitations of Wikipedia relative to other existing, human-curated resources of knowledge; derivative resources, created by converting semi-structured content in Wikipedia into structured data; the role of Wikipedia and its derivatives in text analysis; and the role of Wikipedia and its derivatives in enhancing information retrieval.

2 Tutorial Outline

- Open-domain knowledge and its impact in text analysis and information retrieval;
- Knowledge within, and resources derived from, Wikipedia;
- Role in text analysis: information extraction and beyond.

3 Instructor

Marius Paşca is a research scientist at Google. Current research interests include the acquisition of factual information from unstructured text within documents and queries and its applications to Web search.

Proceedings of COLING 2016, the 26th International Conference on Computational Linguistics: Tutorial Abstracts, page 22, Osaka, Japan, December 11-17 2016.

Association for Computational Linguistics
209 N. Eighth Street
Stroudsburg, Pennsylvania 18360

ISBN 978-1-5108-3338-8

9 781510 833388

CURRAN ASSOCIATES INC.
proceedings.com